ANONYMOUS

Melodies Behind the Mask

Contents

1

Gilded Cage

Crystal chandeliers drip with a cold, artificial light,
   casting fractured diamonds across a polished marble floor.
   Here, in this palace built of wealth and stifling might,
   a gilded cage confines a spirit wanting more.

Silken drapes, heavy with secrets untold,
   frame a world where whispers dance on gilded frames.
   Perfect posture, practiced smiles, stories unfold
   in the suffocating silence of orchestrated games.

Lessons learned in etiquette, a symphony of "shoulds,"
   a carefully curated life, a script meticulously penned.
   Emotions bottled tight, a heart misunderstood,
   a yearning for a world beyond this gilded pretend.

Fingers trace the bars, unseen, a silent, yearning plea,
   to escape this gilded cage, to finally be free.
   Melodies locked within, yearning to be heard,
   a symphony of dreams, waiting to be stirred.

Each practiced note a whisper, a rebellion in disguise,
    a secret language spoken beneath emotionless eyes.
    The grand piano gleams, a silent confidante's embrace,
    a canvas waiting for the storm to take its place.

One day, the melody will rise, a fierce and defiant song,
    shattering the crystal silence, where it has dwelled for long.
    The gilded cage will tremble, its bars will start to bend,
    as the soul within awakens, ready to ascend.

2

Silent Symphony

The hush of a grand estate settles like dust in the air,
   a symphony of secrets held captive, a burden to bear.
   Sunlight bleeds through heavy drapes, painting squares on
the floor,
   illuminating a gilded cage where dreams yearn for more.

A young heart beats a silent rhythm, a counterpoint to the norm,
   a melody yearning to break free from the impending storm.
   Fingers, taught to hold a teacup, twitch with a hidden desire,
   to caress the cool ivory keys, set the soul on fire.

Each practiced piano lesson, a rebellion veiled in grace,
   notes meticulously played, a mask upon her face.
   Scales and sonatas, a language she doesn't speak,
   a yearning for improvisation, a melody wild and unique.

In the quiet corners, when shadows lengthen and grow,
   stolen moments are seized, letting the true feelings flow.
   The grand piano stands silent, a confidante in the night,

as fingers dance on the keys, bathed in the moon's pale light.

A secret symphony unfolds, a torrent of emotions unchained,
furious scales mimicking anger, a yearning melody for what's untamed.
Melancholy chords whisper of sadness, a longing for a life unknown,
while triumphant crescendos echo a spirit that won't be overthrown.

The melody swells, a tempestuous sea, crashing against the gilded walls,
a symphony of defiance that echoes through cavernous halls.
Each note a brushstroke on the canvas of her soul,
a vibrant tapestry woven where conformity takes its toll.

The silence that suffocates by day becomes a canvas at night,
a space where dreams take flight, and emotions ignite.
The young heart beats a rhythm wild, a counterpoint to the norm,
a silent symphony yearning to break free from the impending storm.

Years flicker by, a blur of expectations and polite charades,
a gilded cage of etiquette, where individuality fades.
But the music within persists, a fire that refuses to die,
a secret symphony waiting for the day it can finally fly.

3

Cracked Porcelain

The porcelain doll sits perched upon the shelf,
  a picture-perfect image, a vision of wealth.
  Her smile, a flawless curve, eyes painted blue,
  a masterpiece of expectations, forever meant to stay true.

Her dress, a cascade of lace, a crown upon her head,
  a symbol of refinement, a life flawlessly tread.
  But beneath the polished surface, a hidden fracture lies,
  a crack in the facade, where a different spirit cries.

The young girl who inhabits this gilded cage of pretence,
  yearns for a life less scripted, a world with more expanse.
  She dreams of emotions freely expressed, of laughter unre-
hearsed,
  of melodies bursting forth, a symphony to be versed.

The lessons drilled into her, like porcelain etched with care,
  speak of posture and decorum, a life beyond compare.
  Stiff upper lip and measured words, a smile that never bends,

a carefully crafted image, where true feeling transcends.

But the music within her, a wild and untamed beast,
chafes against the confines, yearning to be released.
The practiced piano scales, a cage for her true song,
a yearning for improvisation, where emotions belong.

In stolen moments, bathed in the moonlight's glow,
the porcelain doll sheds her mask, letting the real feelings
flow.
Fingers dance across the keys, a language understood,
a symphony of rebellion, a yearning misunderstood.

The crack in the facade widens, a whisper turns to a shout,
a defiant melody erupts, tearing the silence out.
The porcelain doll trembles, the image starts to fade,
as the girl within awakens, a spirit unafraid.

The world may see perfection, a flawless form on display,
but beneath the cracks and fractures, a different story will
play.
For the music within her, a force that cannot be tamed,
will shatter the porcelain cage, and a new self will be named.

4

Rebellious in Red

The world sees crimson as a color of fire,
of passion and fury, a burning desire.
For her, it's a rebellion, a flag unfurled,
against the pale expectations of a gilded world.

Her wardrobe, a symphony of muted tones,
beige and cream, a canvas of whispered moans.
A life painted in pastels, a portrait so bland,
a yearning for boldness, a defiant stand.

But in the quiet corners, where shadows reside,
a hint of rebellion, a secret she can't hide.
A single crimson scarf, a whisper of might,
a spark of defiance in the fading light.

The fabric, a whisper against her skin,
a promise of freedom, a battle to win.
It drapes across her shoulders, a shield from the norm,
a symbol of strength in the coming storm.

The grand piano awaits, a battlefield of keys,
    where practiced scales morph into wild melodies.
    Fingers, once hesitant, now dance with a fire,
    painting emotions in crimson, a song of her desire.

The notes cascade down, a torrent of red,
    anger and frustration, long held in her head.
    A crescendo of defiance, a shattering sound,
    the gilded cage trembling, where silence once crowned.

The melody crescendos, a rebellious roar,
    tearing down expectations at life's very core.
    The red scarf a banner, a symbol unfurled,
    against the pale constraints of a stifled world.

Shedding the pastels, the colors so tame,
    embracing the crimson, a soul finally aflame.
    No longer a whisper, a voice clear and bold,
    a symphony of rebellion, a story untold.

5

Untamed Piano

The grand piano, a polished beast of black,
   gleams in the corner, a silent attack.
   Its teeth, a row of ivory keys so white,
   beckon with a promise, a thrilling fight.

Years of practiced scales, a cage for a song,
   a melody yearning to break free, to belong.
   Fingers forced into form, a stifled refrain,
   a yearning for passion, a chance to unleash the rain.

But the lessons recede, a memory dim,
   as a fire ignites within, a wild, untamed hymn.
   The girl at the keyboard, a warrior in disguise,
   with eyes ablaze, and a spirit that flies.

Muscles tense, a battle cry in her soul,
   fingers strike the keys, taking control.
   The practiced notes dissolve, a forgotten score,
   as emotions take flight, bursting forth to the core.

Fury crashes down in a thunderous chord,
    a pent-up frustration, a long-ignored word.
    Melodic tears cascade, a sorrowful plea,
    a yearning for freedom, for a world to finally see.

The piano roars, a tempestuous sea,
    chords crashing and churning, a symphony wild and free.
    Dissonance and harmony dance in a chaotic embrace,
    a reflection of turmoil, a journey with no set pace.

But within the chaos, a melody takes form,
    a whisper of hope weathering the coming storm.
    A gentle arpeggio, a moment of peace,
    a fragile flower blooming amidst the fierce release.

The untamed piano sings, a story untold,
    of a spirit awakened, brave and bold.
    No longer a prisoner, a puppet on strings,
    the girl at the keyboard, the music she sings.

6

Whispers Behind Walls

The opulent mansion, a fortress of stone,
 hides secrets and silence, a world of its own.
 Within its thick walls, whispers take flight,
 stories untold in the fading light.

The girl with the music locked deep in her soul,
 walks through these halls, playing a preordained role.
 A perfect facade, a smile etched in place,
 a carefully crafted image, a gilded disgrace.

But behind the grandeur, in corners unseen,
 whispers of rebellion, a simmering scene.
 The housekeeper, a kind soul with eyes that hold wisdom,
 witnesses the girl's struggle, a silent kingdom.

In hushed tones, stories are shared, dreams take flight,
 a melody sung in the shadows of night.
 The girl confesses her longing, a yearning to break free,
 from the gilded cage, a symphony waiting to be.

The housekeeper listens with a heart full of grace,
    offering solace and comfort in this lonely space.
    She speaks of hidden talents, passions unknown,
    a world of music waiting, a seed to be sown.

"In the quiet hours," she whispers so low,
    "let the music flow, let your true colors show."
    With a knowing smile and a twinkle in her eye,
    she unlocks a secret, a chance to fly.

A dusty piano, hidden in the attic's embrace,
    its keys yellowed with age, a forgotten space.
    The girl ascends the stairs, a hesitant stride,
    a world of possibilities waiting to confide.

Fingers touch the ivory, cool and worn,
    a silent promise whispered, a new day to be born.
    Notes tentative at first, a melody shy,
    then crescendoing with passion, reaching for the sky.

The music fills the attic, a symphony untold,
    emotions unburdened, a story to unfold.
    The whispers behind walls, a secret no more,
    transform into a song, reaching every door.

The melody echoes through the grand halls below,
    a defiance against the status quo.
    The girl, no longer a puppet, her voice finally rings,
    shattering the silence, the music she sings.

The housekeeper smiles, a tear in her eye,

witnessing the birth of a dream soaring high.
For within the whispers, behind the cold walls,
a symphony of freedom triumphantly calls.

13

7

Letters Burned, Dreams Unfurled

The flickering flames of the fireplace cast dancing shadows on
the wall,
 illuminating a scene of quiet rebellion, a secret ritual for all.
 In her hand, she clutches a stack of crisp, white paper,
 each one a testament to a yearning heart, a silent escaper.

These are not love letters, penned with flowery prose,
 but letters of defiance, against the life she loathes.
 Words scrawled in anger, frustration, and despair,
 aimed at the ones who built the gilded cage, who never
seemed to care.

A letter to her mother, a portrait of cold perfection,
 a woman who molded her daughter with a rigid affection.
 "You taught me to smile, but never to laugh," the words accuse,
 "You built a dollhouse of expectations, denying me my muse."

A letter to her father, a distant, aloof figure,
 lost in the labyrinth of work, a love that never would linger.

"You saw potential, but never my soul," the ink cries out,
"You groomed me for a future I never chose, a path filled with
doubt."

Tears stain the paper, blurring the lines of blame,
    a lifetime of silence finally finding its name.
    Each sentence a brushstroke, painting a picture untold,
    of a young spirit yearning, a story waiting to unfold.

But amidst the anger, a flicker of hope ignites,
    a dream taking flight, bathed in the fire's gentle lights.
    A letter to herself, a promise whispered low,
    to break free from the chains, and watch her true colors flow.

"You are not a possession," the words fiercely proclaim,
    "You are a symphony waiting to be played, a melody with a
name."
    The dreams she locked away, hidden beneath the facade,
    are now unveiled on paper, a path she'll finally tread.

With a trembling hand, she feeds the letters to the flames,
    watching them transform, their message carried by the
flames.
    The ashes rise, a symbol of letting go,
    of burning down the past, to plant seeds of what she'll grow.

The fire crackles, a symphony of its own,
    echoing the transformation that's slowly being sown.
    The embers glow, a promise warm and bright,
    of a future filled with music, and a future taking flight.

The girl stands tall, her eyes reflecting the fire's light,
a newfound resolve burning with an unwavering might.
The letters may be gone, their words etched in her soul,
a roadmap to freedom, making her story whole.

The gilded cage still stands, but its bars seem to bend,
as the girl with dreams unfurled steps forward, ready to ascend.

8

Shadows on Silk

Opulence drapes the room in a heavy embrace,
  silk tapestries whisper secrets on the fireplace's warm face.
  Sunlight struggles to pierce the thick, velvet drapes,
  casting long shadows that dance in languorous shapes.

Here, she sits, a picture of porcelain grace,
  a carefully crafted image, a mask upon her face.
  Fingers rest idly in her lap, a practiced pose,
  but beneath the surface, a wild melody grows.

The piano beckons from the corner, a silent invitation,
  to break free from the shadows, defy the expectation.
  Its polished surface gleams, a promise untold,
  of a world where emotions bloom, and stories unfold.

But the air hangs heavy with unspoken commands,
  a symphony of etiquette played by unseen hands.
  Straight posture, a measured smile, a voice soft and low,
  the stifling weight of expectations, a constant undertow.

She yearns to unleash the tempest raging inside,
    to paint the walls with a symphony, let her true colors confide.
    But fear whispers doubts in a serpent's embrace,
    of disapproval and judgment, a fall from her place.

The shadows on the silk dance in mocking glee,
    a reflection of the turmoil hidden for all to see.
    They twist and contort, forming grotesque shapes,
    mocking her yearning, highlighting her escapes.

Each creak of the floorboard, a heartbeat's loud boom,
    amplifying the silence in this opulent tomb.
    Will she ever break free from this gilded cocoon?
    Will her melody ever be sung, beneath the harvest moon?

But then, a flicker of defiance ignites in her eye,
    a spark of rebellion that refuses to die.
    She straightens her spine, a newfound resolve takes hold,
    the shadows on the silk begin to lose their hold.

Fingers reach out, trembling at first, then bold and sure,
    grazing the cool ivory keys, a melody to procure.
    A single note rings out, a tentative sound,
    shattering the silence, claiming the hallowed ground.

The shadows recoil, surprised and subdued,
    as the music takes flight, powerful and crude.
    It carries anger and frustration, a yearning to be free,
    a chaotic symphony breaking from her misery.

The notes flow faster, a torrent of emotion unleashed,

painting a portrait of turmoil, a story finally preached.
The shadows on the silk dance to a different tune,
a melody of rebellion beneath the afternoon moon.

The room transforms, bathed in a vibrant light,
as she surrenders to the music, taking flight.
No longer a prisoner of shadows and silk,
she becomes the melody, her true self unveiled.

9

The Housekeeper's Lullaby

The hush of twilight descends on the grand estate,
   casting long shadows that whisper and wait.
   In a room tucked away, unseen and unheard,
   a symphony of comfort, a gentle word.

The housekeeper, a woman with eyes that hold time,
   sits by the bedside, a soothing rhyme.
   The young girl, restless and filled with despair,
   tosses beneath the covers, a burden to bear.

"What troubles you, child?" the housekeeper asks,
   her voice a warm blanket, dispelling the tasks.
   The girl hesitates, a damsel in distress,
   a story untold, a hidden wilderness.

With a trembling voice, she spills her woes,
   of expectations unmet, dreams turned to foes.
   The gilded cage, a prison of gold,
   where emotions are stifled, stories untold.

The housekeeper listens, a patient embrace,
a silent sanctuary in this lonely space.
With gentle hands, she smooths the girl's hair,
offering solace, a burden to share.

"There's music within you," the housekeeper sighs,
"a melody waiting to take to the skies."
She speaks of a hidden piano, a secret delight,
a world of creation bathed in moonlight.

"In the quiet hours, when shadows reside,"
she whispers softly, with a love that can't hide,
"let the music flow, let your feelings take flight,
and paint your emotions in the pale moonlight."

A lullaby hums, a melody wise,
of resilience and hope, that forever will rise.
The girl closes her eyes, the tension unwinds,
as the housekeeper's song soothes the troubled minds.

The lullaby echoes, a promise untold,
of a world where dreams bloom, braver and bold.
The girl drifts to sleep, a calmness descends,
knowing the housekeeper's love, a journey that transcends.

For within the silence, a bond takes its hold,
a symphony of understanding, more precious than gold.
The housekeeper, a beacon in the night's embrace,
empowers the girl, to find her own space.

The lullaby fades, but its melody stays,

a whisper of courage for brighter days.
The girl awakens, a newfound resolve,
to break free from the cage, and watch her spirit evolve.

10

Masks We Wear

A masquerade ball unfolds, a spectacle of disguise,
  where hidden identities dance beneath fabricated skies.
  Silk masks adorned with jewels, feathers, and lace,
  conceal emotions and secrets, a game with no face.

She moves through the throng, a porcelain doll dressed in white,
  a perfect facade, a practiced smile, reflecting the night.
  Her eyes, hidden behind a mask of painted glee,
  long for authenticity, a yearning to finally be free.

The ballroom waltz swirls, a dizzying display,
  of couples twirling, emotions kept at bay.
  But beneath the laughter, a hollowness resides,
  a yearning for connection, where truth truly confides.

The mask feels heavy, a suffocating weight,
  a constant reminder of the life she must create.
  A symphony of emotions locked deep within,
  yearning to be heard, to pierce through the din.

As the music swells, a waltz turns to a tango's fire,
   a flicker of rebellion, a spark of desire.
   Her steps falter, the mask slips a touch,
   revealing a glimpse of the girl she loved so much.

A stranger approaches, his eyes meet hers through the veil,
   a flicker of recognition, a whispered tale.
   They dance in silence, a language unspoken,
   a connection forged, where masks are awoken.

He sees the fire in her eyes, the yearning beneath,
   a kindred spirit seeking solace, a chance to breathe.
   In a hushed tone, he murmurs, "Let the mask fall away,
   reveal the music within, let your true self play."

The music crescendos, a chaotic embrace,
   a reflection of the turmoil within this gilded space.
   Hesitantly, she reaches up, a trembling hand,
   and brushes the mask aside, taking a fearless stand.

The ballroom gasps, a collective surprise,
   as the girl beneath the mask confronts unveiled lies.
   But a smile graces her lips, no longer a mask's decree,
   a genuine expression, finally feeling free.

The music slows, a tender melody takes hold,
   a shared moment of truth, a story yet untold.
   The masquerade ball fades, a distant charade,
   as they walk away together, a future unafraid.

For the masks may have fallen, revealing the truth within,

but the music will continue, a symphony to begin.
No longer a prisoner of societal pretence,
she embraces her true self, a magnificent resonance.

11

Scissors and Shadows

The glint of polished steel catches the morning light,
a pair of sharp scissors, a symbol of hidden might.
In her hand they rest, more than just a tool,
a whisper of rebellion, a defiance uncool.

They've snipped away fabric, creating a perfect facade,
transforming her into a doll, never truly bad.
Lace and silk, a gilded cage she's forced to wear,
a constant reminder of the burdens she must bear.

But the scissors hold a secret, a yearning untold,
a desire to cut deeper, than fabric or fold.
To sever the ties that bind her, the expectations that choke,
and finally unleash the symphony, her spirit evokes.

The shadows on the wall dance in a macabre ballet,
mocking reflections of the life she can't display.
They twist and contort, a distorted display,
of potential caged, dreams fading away.

But the scissors glint defiance, a promise held tight,
to sever the shadows, and claim back the light.
With a determined hand, she makes a bold slice,
through the tapestry of expectations, a defiant device.

The shadows recoil, surprised and subdued,
as the sunlight streams in, a story renewed.
The gilded cage trembles, its bars start to bend,
as the girl with the scissors, prepares to ascend.

The sharp blades whisper a message, a symphony's call,
to dismantle the structures, that cause her to fall.
They'll snip away doubts, and sever the fear,
ushering in a future, bold and clear.

But the scissors are not just for destruction they hold,
a power to create, a narrative yet untold.
They can sculpt and refine, with a practiced hand,
a melody waiting, to rise from the sand.

With a newfound purpose, she cuts and she shapes,
notes and chords dance, escaping their capes.
The scissors transform, from weapon to pen,
composing a future, where dreams can begin.

The symphony swells, a defiant roar,
tearing down expectations at life's very core.
The glint of the scissors, a beacon so bright,
a symbol of courage, and a future taking flight.

12

Cracks in the Facade

Sunlight bleeds through heavy drapes, a hesitant guest,
   illuminating a world where secrets are dressed
   in layers of silence, a facade meticulously built,
   a gilded cage where emotions remain wilfully spilt.

Beneath the polished surface, a tremor takes hold,
   a crack in the facade, a story untold.
   Years of practiced smiles, a mask carefully worn,
   begin to crumble, as a new feeling is born.

The melody within, a symphony long suppressed,
   yearns to break free, a yearning confessed.
   Scales and sonatas, mere echoes of the past,
   a hollow refrain, that cannot forever last.

The music locked within, a torrent unseen,
   churns beneath the surface, a rebellious queen.
   Fingers, trained for poise, twitch with a hidden desire,
   to caress the cool ivory keys, set the soul on fire.

In stolen moments, bathed in the moonlight's glow,
a secret rebellion, a symphony takes its flow.
Piano keys whisper, stories they impart,
a language of emotions, a yearning for a new start.

The melody unfolds, a tempestuous tide,
painting emotions in passionate stride.
Anger and frustration, a long-held despair,
erupt in a crescendo, shattering the sterile air.

The music crescendos, a defiant roar,
tearing down expectations at life's very core.
The crack in the facade widens, the image starts to bend,
as the spirit within awakens, a journey without end.

The world may see perfection, a flawless display,
but beneath the cracks and fractures, a different story will
play.
For the music within her, a force that cannot be tamed,
will shatter the gilded cage, and a new self will be named.

The facade may crumble, revealing the truth unseen,
a symphony of defiance, where dreams can finally convene.
The crack in the surface, a spark that ignites,
a journey of self-discovery, bathed in the music's bright lights.

13

Unexpected Melody

The weight of expectations, a heavy, gilded crown,
   presses down upon her, a burden that weighs her down.
   Years of meticulous training, a script meticulously penned,
   leave no room for dissonance, no room for a world to
transcend.

The grand piano sits silent, a monument of control,
   its keys a battlefield of practiced scales, taking their toll.
   Each carefully played note, a whisper of conformity's hold,
   a yearning for improvisation, a story yet untold.

But in the quiet corners, where shadows softly creep,
   a melody unexpected, begins to gently seep.
   A single note, hesitant at first, a tentative sound,
   breaks the silence, a rebellion on sacred ground.

It's not a practiced phrase, nor a melody learned by rote,
   but a whisper of the heart, a surge of a hidden note.
   Fingers dance on the keys, a language understood,

a symphony of emotions, yearning to be imbued.

The unexpected melody, a tapestry unfolds,
    of dreams long suppressed, and stories untold.
    It paints a world of wonder, where colors freely flow,
    and replaces expectations with a vibrant, soulful glow.

The girl, once a puppet, controlled by unseen hands,
    embraces the melody, a spirit that expands.
    The unexpected notes, a defiance unfurled,
    shattering the silence of a controlled, gilded world.

The melody grows bolder, a crescendo takes flight,
    a symphony of freedom, bathed in the pale moonlight.
    The weight of expectations seems to slowly wane,
    replaced by the power of a self-composed strain.

The unexpected melody, a beacon so bright,
    illuminates the darkness, chasing away the night.
    It becomes a promise, a whispered decree,
    to break free from the cage, and finally be.

The girl with the unexpected melody, a voice newly found,
    will rewrite the script, on a new and fertile ground.
    No longer bound by expectations, a life preordained,
    she embraces the music, a future beautifully refrained.

14

The Storm Within

A tempest brews within the confines of her soul,
a churning sea of emotions, taking their toll.
Years of stifled expression, a dam holding tight,
threaten to burst with fury, under the pale moonlight.

The gilded cage she inhabits, a symphony of pretense,
echoes with practiced laughter, devoid of true essence.
The perfect facade, meticulously maintained,
hides a restless spirit, forever chained.

The grand piano, a silent sentinel stands,
its polished surface a reflection of barren lands.
Notes practiced and perfect, devoid of true flight,
a melody yearning to break free into the night.

But the storm within gathers, a force undeniable,
cracks appear in the facade, previously unviable.
A single tear rolls down, a glistening cascade,
a prelude to the tempest, soon to be displayed.

Fingers tremble on the keys, a hesitant touch,
   a tentative note escapes, a yearning too much.
   Then another, and another, a chaotic cascade,
   a symphony of rebellion, a storm serenade.

The music explodes, a torrent of sound,
   anger and frustration, unleashed and unbound.
   Melodies writhe and twist, in a tempestuous dance,
   a reflection of the turmoil, given a fleeting glance.

The gilded cage trembles, as the storm rages on,
   the bars begin to bend, with a defiant, mournful song.
   The practiced scales and sonatas, fade into the night,
   replaced by a primal scream, bathed in pale moonlight.

The storm within her rages, a cathartic release,
   emotions long pent-up, finally finding peace.
   Tears flow freely, cleansing the pain within,
   as the music carries the burden, on a mournful violin.

But amidst the chaos, a melody takes form,
   a whisper of hope weathering the coming storm.
   A gentle arpeggio, a moment of grace,
   a fragile flower blooming, in this tempestuous space.

The storm within her subsides, leaving a gentle breeze,
   a symphony transformed, carried on the seas.
   The gilded cage may stand, but its power feels thin,
   as the girl with the music, prepares to rise within.

The tempest has cleansed her, a baptism of sound,

a newfound strength awakened, on sacred ground.
She embraces the storm within, a part of her core,
a symphony of resilience, forevermore.

15

Symphony of Secrets

The grand estate whispers secrets in the rustling leaves,
   stories etched in shadows, on moonlit, wind-swept eaves.
   Within its hallowed halls, a melody resides,
   a symphony of secrets, where truth forever hides.

She walks the polished floors, a phantom in disguise,
   a picture of perfection, with sorrow in her eyes.
   Her smile, a practiced curve, a mask impeccably worn,
   concealing a symphony of dreams, a spirit newly born.

The weight of expectations, a gilded, crushing crown,
   forces a graceful posture, a life her own, not found.
   Lessons of etiquette, a script meticulously penned,
   leave no room for dissonance, a world without end.

But in the quiet corners, when shadows dance and play,
   a melody forbidden, begins to find its way.
   Fingers brush the surface, of a dusty, hidden key,
   unlocking a chamber, where emotions yearn to be free.

35

The attic, a forgotten realm, bathed in twilight's embrace,
   holds a grand piano, a sanctuary in this sterile space.
   Its ivory keys whisper tales, of forgotten dreams unfurled,
   a symphony of secrets, waiting to be heard.

Hesitantly, she sits, a touch both light and shy,
   and with a tentative note, the melody starts to fly.
   Scales, forgotten and faded, replaced by raw emotion,
   a cascade of feelings, a passionate devotion.

The music swells and surges, a tempestuous sea,
   anger and frustration, yearning to finally be free.
   Melodies intertwine, a tapestry of despair,
   a symphony of secrets, filling the stagnant air.

Each note a brushstroke, painting a vivid scene,
   of a caged spirit yearning, for a life yet unseen.
   The secrets of the estate, whispered on the breeze,
   echo in the music, carried by the rustling leaves.

The weight of generations, a burden she must bear,
   finds solace in the music, a release beyond compare.
   The symphony of secrets, a cathartic cry,
   shatters the silence, reaching for the open sky.

With each powerful chord, the walls begin to bend,
   the gilded cage falters, a story without end.
   The girl with the music, no longer a puppet on strings,
   embraces her true voice, the melody she sings.

The hidden symphony, a beacon in the night,

illuminates the darkness, with a passionate light.
The secrets of the past, transformed into song,
become a bridge to freedom, where she can finally belong.

And as the last note fades, a sense of peace descends,
the symphony of secrets, finding its happy ends.
The girl with the music, a spirit bold and bright,
prepares to rewrite the future, bathed in the morning's light.

16

The Language of Moonlight

The moon, a silent witness, bathes the grand estate in silver,
    casting long shadows that dance and quiver.
    Inside, a restless spirit, yearning to be free,
    seeks solace in the language of the moonlit melody.

The gilded cage, once a symbol of wealth and control,
    now feels suffocating, a story untold.
    The girl within, a prisoner of expectations' hold,
    yearns to break free, her true colors unfold.

The grand piano gleams, a beacon in the night,
    its ivory keys whispering secrets of hidden might.
    Years of practiced scales, a faded refrain,
    give way to a symphony, born of moonlight's gentle rain.

Fingers, once hesitant, now dance with newfound grace,
    composing a language, etched on the moonlit space.
    Melodies flow freely, unbound by any rule,
    a symphony of emotions, breaking every cool.

The language of moonlight, a tapestry so bright,
   weaves tales of frustration and dreams taking flight.
   Anger and sorrow, in perfect harmony entwined,
   a reflection of the turmoil, a restless spirit confined.

Each note a brushstroke, painting a vibrant scene,
   of a caged bird yearning, for a world evergreen.
   The melody crescendos, a defiant roar,
   shattering the silence, a truth forevermore.

The moonbeams dance, a celestial ballet,
   mirroring the emotions, the music holds at bay.
   The gilded cage trembles, its bars begin to bend,
   as the girl with the music, prepares to ascend.

The language of moonlight, a symphony so grand,
   transforms the nightingale's song, across the silent land.
   It becomes a promise, a whispered decree,
   to break free from the cage, and finally be.

The girl with the music, a voice newly found,
   will rewrite the script, on a new and fertile ground.
   No longer bound by expectations, a life preordained,
   she embraces the language of moonlight, forever unchained.

And as the last note fades, a gentle peace descends,
   the moonbeams a witness, to a journey that transcends.
   The girl with the music, a spirit bold and bright,
   prepares to rewrite the future, bathed in the moon's gentle
light.

The language of moonlight, a legacy will hold,
a symphony of freedom, a story to be told.
A reminder to all, with a spirit that burns,
to break free from the cage, and let their true light return.

17

The Firebird's Flight

Within the grand estate, a gilded prison vast,
    A restless spirit slumbers, a melody unsurpassed.
    Expectations, a heavy cloak, a role meticulously played,
    But beneath the polished surface, a yearning fire is laid.

The grand piano stands silent, a monument of control,
    A battlefield of practiced scales, taking their silent toll.
    Each note a measured whisper, devoid of vibrant flight,
    A yearning for improvisation, a symphony bathed in light.

But in the quiet corners, where shadows softly creep,
    A spark ignites, a slumbering dream begins to leap.
    A melody unexpected, a whisper in the night,
    A symphony of defiance, a firebird taking flight.

Fingers, once hesitant, now dance with newfound grace,
    Composing a language, etched on the moonlit space.
    Melodies flow freely, unbound by any rule,
    A symphony of emotions, breaking every cool.

The music explodes, a torrent of sound,
　　Shattering the silence, where secrets abound.
　　Anger and frustration, in a passionate display,
　　A firebird's fury, scorching the gilded way.

The gilded cage trembles, as the melody takes hold,
　　The bars begin to bend, a story yet untold.
　　The practiced scales and sonatas, fade into the past,
　　Replaced by a primal scream, a symphony built to last.

The firebird's flight, a dazzling display,
　　Wings of music soaring, chasing the night away.
　　It paints a world of wonder, where dreams ignite and burn,
　　A symphony of rebellion, a future yet to learn.

The melody crescendos, a defiant roar,
　　Shattering the silence of a controlled, gilded core.
　　The weight of expectations crumbles and falls away,
　　Replaced by the power of a self-composed, vibrant lay.

The firebird's song, a beacon so bright,
　　Illuminates the darkness, setting the future alight.
　　It becomes a promise, a whispered decree,
　　To break free from the cage, and finally be.

The girl with the music, a voice newly found,
　　Will rewrite the script, on a fertile, boundless ground.
　　No longer bound by expectations, a life preordained,
　　She embraces the firebird's flight, forever unchained.

And as the last note fades, a transformation takes hold,

The firebird's embers glow, a story yet to unfold.
The girl with the music, a spirit bold and free,
Soars above the gilded cage, for eternity.

18

Echoes in the Hall of Mirrors

The grand hall gleams, a labyrinth of glass,
reflecting distorted visions, a never-ending mass.
Each mirror a canvas, painting a fractured view,
of a life preordained, a gilded cage, ever true.

She walks the polished floor, a phantom in disguise,
a reflection of expectations, in her downcast eyes.
A smile, a practiced mask, a role meticulously played,
a symphony of silence, a dream forever delayed.

The weight of generations, a burden she must bear,
echoes in the mirrors, a whispered, haunting prayer.
Lessons of etiquette, a script meticulously penned,
leave no room for dissonance, a future without end.

But a flicker of defiance, ignites in her soul,
a yearning for freedom, to break free from control.
A melody forgotten, whispers on the breeze,
a symphony of secrets, carried through the trees.

In the quiet corners, where shadows softly creep,
a dusty piano slumbers, secrets it holds deep.
Its ivory keys silent, yearning for a touch,
to break the spell of mirrors, and sing out so much.

Hesitantly, she approaches, a breath caught in her throat,
fingers brushing the surface, a long-forgotten note.
The sound, a gentle whisper, a tear rolls down her face,
awakening the echoes, in this mirrored, sterile space.

The melody unfolds, a tapestry of sound,
of dreams long suppressed, on sacred ground.
Anger and frustration, a yearning to be seen,
shatter the mirrored illusion, a world evergreen.

Each note a brushstroke, painting a vibrant scene,
of a caged spirit yearning, for a life serene.
The music swells and surges, a defiant roar,
shattering the silence, forevermore.

The mirrors tremble, as the symphony takes hold,
the reflections distort, a story yet untold.
The practiced smiles and postures, begin to melt away,
replaced by the raw emotions, of a brand new day.

The melody transforms, a bridge across the hall,
connecting fractured images, ready to enthrall.
The echoes intertwine, a chorus of release,
a symphony of acceptance, finding inner peace.

No longer a prisoner, of a reflected lie,

she embraces the mirrors, with a newfound cry.
For in each distorted image, a truth begins to gleam,
a symphony of self-discovery, a beautiful, waking dream.

The hall of mirrors, a transformed domain,
no longer a prison, but a canvas to reclaim.
With every note she plays, the reflections bend,
a symphony of acceptance, until the very end.

And as the last note fades, a sense of freedom rings,
the girl with the music, a butterfly with wings.
She soars above the mirrors, a spirit light and bright,
embracing her melody, bathed in the morning's light.

19

Escape Symphony

The air hangs heavy, thick with stifled dreams,
    A gilded cage of comfort, where nothing truly gleams.
    Expectations, like bars, a gilded prison vast,
    Hold captive a yearning spirit, a melody unsurpassed.

The grand piano sits silent, a monument of control,
    Where practiced scales and sonatas take their silent toll.
    Each note a measured whisper, a hollow, lifeless sound,
    Yearning for improvisation, a symphony unbound.

But in the quiet corners, where shadows softly creep,
    A spark ignites, a hidden fire begins to leap.
    A melody unexpected, a whisper in the night,
    A symphony of defiance, a yearning for flight.

The first note trembles, hesitant and shy,
    A tentative escape, a tear in the gilded sky.
    Fingers dance on the keys, a language yet unknown,
    A symphony of longing, a seed about to be sown.

The music swells and surges, a tide that breaks the hold,
  Shattering the silence, a story yet untold.
  Anger and frustration, a torrent loud and clear,
  Shattering the facade, casting off years of fear.

The gilded cage reverberates, the bars begin to bend,
  As the melody takes hold, a journey without end.
  The practiced scales and sonatas, fade into the past,
  Replaced by a primal scream, a symphony built to last.

The melody transforms, with each resounding beat,
  A map unfolds, a path to freedom, bittersweet.
  Each note a brushstroke, painting a vibrant scene,
  Of a world beyond the cage, lush and evergreen.

Memories bittersweet, in harmonies they weave,
  A tapestry of gratitude, for lessons learned and leave.
  But the future beckons, a symphony bold and bright,
  A promise whispered, bathed in the moon's gentle light.

The final chord resonates, a triumphant sigh,
  The gilded cage crumbles, beneath the open sky.
  The weight of expectations, a burden cast aside,
  The girl with the music, finally takes her stride.

With each echoing note, the path becomes more clear,
  A symphony of courage, dispelling every fear.
  The world awaits her music, a story yet to write,
  An escape symphony, bathed in the morning's light.

She walks towards the horizon, a newfound strength within,

The melody within her, a never-ending din.
A testament to the power, of a yearning set alight,
The escape symphony, soaring into the endless night.

20

Empty Applause

The spotlight pierces, a harsh and blinding gaze,
Illuminating a stage, a carefully crafted maze.
A symphony of movements, practiced with such care,
But the audience's applause, leaves a hollowness to bear.

The polished smile she wears, a mask meticulously made,
Hides a churning discontent, a yearning that's betrayed.
For the notes that truly sing, the melodies within,
Remain unheard, unseen, a symphony of unseen sin.

They clap for dazzling tricks, for feats of strength and grace,
But the rawest parts of her, find no echo in this space.
The music of her soul, a language all its own,
Is met with vacant stares, a symphony unknown.

She pirouettes and leaps, a puppet on a string,
Performing for their pleasure, the joy they seem to bring.
But the emptiness within, a cavern vast and deep,
Echoes with the silence, where her true feelings sleep.

The final bow is struck, the curtain slowly falls,
  The thunderous applause, a hollow sound that galls.
  For in their fleeting praise, no true connection lies,
  Just empty validation, in their unfeeling eyes.

They see a flawless dancer, a picture-perfect scene,
  But not the scars of passion, the struggles that have been.
  The blood and sweat and tears, poured into every note,
  Lost in the cacophony, of a world that doesn't vote.

She walks away from the stage, the cheers begin to fade,
  A burden in her heart, a truth that can't be swayed.
  The applause may echo, a fleeting, hollow sound,
  But the symphony within her, on sacred ground is found.

For true validation lies, not in the fleeting praise,
  But in the authenticity, of the music that she plays.
  In the raw and honest notes, that only she can hear,
  A symphony of self, dispelling every fear.

One day, she'll find an audience, with hearts that truly see,
  Who'll listen to her music, and set her spirit free.
  But until then, she'll dance, for the melody's own sake,
  And let the empty applause, for her own journey's sake.

The stage may hold her captive, for a moment in this game,
  But the symphony within her, will forever be untamed.

21

The Unseen Stage

The world unfolds in muted tones, a backdrop to her day,
A symphony of obligations, where dreams are tucked away.
Papers stack and deadlines loom, a constant, nagging beat,
But beneath the surface hums a song, a rhythm ever sweet.

The office walls confine her, a sterile, lifeless space,
But within her mind, a stage awaits, a vibrant, hidden place.
The fluorescent lights transform to spotlights, harsh and bright,
And she's no longer filing clerk, but a creature of the night.

In stolen moments, bathed in the glow of a computer screen,
She crafts her costumes, worlds unseen, a vibrant, flowing sheen.
Lunch breaks become rehearsals, lines whispered under breath,
Transforming dull corridors, into stages facing death.

The stapler becomes a scepter, the printer, a grand throne,

Each mundane task a prelude, to a performance of her own.
The click-clack of the keyboard, a rhythmic, driving beat,
As she battles mythical beasts, with a warrior's grace, com-
plete.

The spreadsheets morph to scripts, a story yet untold,
Of love and loss and triumph, a world both brave and bold.
With each typed letter, a character comes alive,
Breathing passions on the page, where her own spirit thrives.

The filing cabinet, a portal, to fantastical domains,
Where she dances with the fairies, and whispers with the
rains.
The photocopier tray, a makeshift balcony's edge,
As she delivers monologues, for a phantom, unseen judge.

The day may seem a drudgery, a never-ending show,
But the unseen stage within her, lets her spirit truly flow.
For in the quiet corners, when the world seems dull and gray,
She finds solace in performance, where her true colors play.

One day, she dreams, the unseen stage will come to light,
The costumes and the characters, bathed in the real spotlight.
But until then, she'll play her part, with passion and with
grace,
The queen of the unseen stage, in a world of her own space.

For the truest performance, isn't measured by acclaim,
But by the fire in the heart, and the burning, endless flame.
And the girl with the hidden stage, will never lose her spark,
A symphony of dreams alive, in the ever-darkening park.

22

Brushstrokes of Freedom

The world a canvas, vast and white, a life yet undefined,
Expectations like shackles, a spirit tightly confined.
A palette filled with muted tones, a script meticulously penned,
But a fierce yearning ignites within, a voice that will transcend.

The brush, a silent weapon, held hesitant at first,
A single stroke, a whispered plea, a universe to burst.
Colors dance and swirl and blend, emotions take their hold,
A symphony of self unleashed, a story yet untold.

On the canvas, dreams take flight, on wings of vibrant hue,
Soaring past the lines of doubt, a world forever new.
Frustration bleeds in crimson strokes, a fiery, burning rage,
Yearning for acceptance, on a life's unturned page.

The muted tones of expectation, slowly fade away,
Replaced by a kaleidoscope, where the spirit chooses to play.

Each brushstroke a rebellion, a defiant, joyous cry,
Shattering the shackles of control, reaching for the open sky.

Flowers bloom in fields of gold, a testament to hope,
While stormy seas in indigo, with hidden struggles cope.
The canvas becomes a mirror, reflecting all within,
A tapestry of emotions, where truth can finally win.

No longer bound by perfect lines, or a world in shades of gray,
The artist paints with reckless joy, for she has found her way.
The brushstrokes dance and sing a song, a symphony so bright,
A masterpiece of self-discovery, bathed in the morning's light.

The world may see a canvas, a spectacle to behold,
But within each vibrant image, a story yet unfolds.
A journey of defiance, a spirit breaking free,
Brushstrokes of liberation, for all the world to see.

For art is not mere aesthetics, nor a practice to refine,
But a language of the soul, a truth forever thine.
The artist with the brush of hope, will forever paint her plea,
A symphony of self-expression, for eternity.

The canvas may be finite, the colors bound to fade,
But the message will endure, a legacy self-made.
A testament to the power, of a spirit unconfined,
Brushstrokes of freedom, forever etched in the mind.

23

The Price of Silence

A gilded cage of porcelain, a smile etched on her face,
  A symphony of secrets, locked in a silent space.
  Years of practiced silence, a wall she built so high,
  Emotions bottled tightly, beneath a tearless sky.

The weight of expectations, a crown upon her head,
  Demanded perfect posture, a life with nothing said.
  Words unspoken, feelings veiled, a tapestry so thin,
  Hiding the storm within her, a turmoil held within.

The grand piano sits silent, its keys a frozen plea,
  Once a symphony of laughter, now a haunting memory.
  Scales practiced with precision, devoid of any soul,
  A hollow, lifeless echo, taking its silent toll.

The girl within the silence, a prisoner of her role,
  Yearns to break free from the script, and finally take control.
  But fear of judgment's sting, keeps her voice tightly bound,
  A symphony of longing, with no release resound.

The silence breeds resentment, a bitterness that grows,
  A slow, insidious poison, where happiness once arose.
  Anger simmers, unaddressed, a festering, hidden sore,
  Turning dreams to ashes, on a barren, lonely shore.

The weight of bottled feelings, a burden hard to bear,
  Manifests in shadows, a haunting, chilling stare.
  Nightmares plague her slumber, whispers in the dark,
  A symphony of torment, leaving an invisible mark.

The gilded cage she inhabits, a prison cold and vast,
  Echoes with the silence, a future meant to last.
  But cracks begin to spider, a tremor deep within,
  The price of silence rising, a battle yet to win.

One day, a tear may fall, a whisper break the hold,
  The dam will burst, unleashing emotions uncontrolled.
  A torrent of anger, frustration, and despair,
  A symphony of the silenced, filling the stagnant air.

But there's another path, a whisper in the night,
  To break the chains of silence, and reclaim her inner light.
  To find a gentle voice, to speak her truth with grace,
  And face the world with courage, a smile upon her face.

The price of silence is heavy, a burden far too steep,
  The girl with the unspoken words, a promise she must keep.
  To find her voice, her music, a symphony to share,
  And break free from the gilded cage, to breathe the open air.

For silence may be easy, a path well-trodden now,

But the symphony within her, deserves a brighter vow.
Let the music be her message, a testament to fight,
Against the price of silence, and reclaim her inner light.

24

Shattering the Cast

The mold, a cage of expectations, cold and hard and gray,
  Cast in the image of another, a path they wouldn't stray.
  Lines etched deep, a rigid form, a life they didn't choose,
  A symphony of conformity, with nothing left to lose.

But a restless spirit stirs within, a yearning to break free,
  To shatter the confining mold, and finally truly be.
  A seed of defiance planted, a whisper in the night,
  A symphony of rebellion, bathed in the pale moonlight.

The world may judge and question, with furrowed brows and
stares,
  But the spirit in the mold, no longer craves their cares.
  For expectations, like shackles, can only hold for so long,
  Before the will to be themself, bursts forth in a defiant song.

The cracks begin to spider, across the rigid form,
  A tremor in the foundation, weathering the coming storm.
  Each doubt, a hammer blow, each fear, a chisel's bite,

Slowly chipping away the mold, to reveal the hidden light.

The world may gasp and sputter, at the sight of what's to come,
    A symphony of self-discovery, a melody yet to be sung.
    The form begins to crumble, the lines begin to fade,
    A new creation rising, emotions unafraid.

The spirit breaks the surface, a butterfly takes flight,
    With wings of vibrant colors, bathed in the morning's light.
    No longer bound by expectations, a life preordained,
    They embrace the unknown future, forever unchained.

The shattered mold, a testament, to the fight within,
    A symphony of courage, where a new journey can begin.
    For breaking free from expectations, isn't a path for the faint,
    But a melody of self-discovery, a beautiful, defiant paint.

The world may hold its breath, at the sight of something new,
    But the spirit that once fit the mold, now soars in skies of
blue.
    A beacon for the dreamers, a testament to the fight,
    That breaking the mold is freedom, bathed in the purest light.

So let the expectations crumble, let the judgments fade away,
    For the symphony within them, deserves to see the day.
    With every shattered fragment, a new creation starts,
    A testament to the power, of brave and open hearts.

25

A World in Black and White

The world unfurls in shades of gray, a tapestry so bleak,
  A symphony of muted tones, where vibrant colors seek
  To peek through cracks in the facade, a whisper in the night,
  But rigid lines and stark commands, extinguish any light.

The grand estate, a monument, to order and control,
  Where every step is measured, a story yet untold.
  The polished floors gleam coldly, reflecting back the same,
  A world devoid of laughter, a never-ending game.

The weight of generations, a burden on her soul,
  A script meticulously penned, a life to take its toll.
  Lessons learned in black and white, a future preordained,
  No room for whimsy, passion, or a fire untamed.

The grand piano stands silent, its keys a mournful choir,
  Each practiced note a whisper, devoid of vibrant fire.
  Scales and sonatas, rigid forms, a symphony of might,
  But the music of her spirit, yearns for a world so bright.

Her dreams, like watercolor hues, bleed on the canvas white,
A yearning for adventure, bathed in the morning's light.
But fear of judgment's harsh gaze, keeps her colors tightly bound,
A symphony of longing, with no release resound.

The world demands perfection, a flawless display of grace,
A smile etched on her features, a mask upon her face.
Emotions bottled tightly, a wellspring deep within,
A silent, raging tempest, where shadows always win.

The weight of expectation, a crushing, heavy cloak,
Stifles every outburst, stifles every joke.
No room for spontaneity, in this world of black and white,
A symphony of silence, devoid of morning's light.

But in the quiet corners, where shadows softly creep,
A spark ignites, a yearning, a promise yet to keep.
A melody forgotten, whispers on the breeze,
A symphony of rebellion, carried through the trees.

The girl with the muted spirit, dreams of a world in bloom,
Where colors dance and shimmer, dispelling life's dark gloom.
One day, she'll break the mold, defy the rigid line,
And paint her world in vibrant hues, a symphony divine.

For the world in black and white, can't hold her forevermore,
The symphony within her, craves a vibrant, open door.
With every whispered note, a flicker of defiance grows,
A world in black and white, will soon explode in rose.

The girl will be the artist, of her own destiny,
   A symphony of color, forever wild and free.
   The world may scoff and question, but she'll paint with all her might,
   And transform the world in black and white, into a dazzling light.

26

A Spark in the Shadows

The grand estate, a marble tomb, where whispers softly roam,
    A symphony of silence, in a world that feels like home.
    A gilded cage of expectations, with bars of polished gold,
    Where every life is preordained, a story yet untold.

She walks the halls, a phantom form, a practiced smile in place,
    A perfect picture, duty-bound, with nary a trace
    Of passion or of fire, the spirit held at bay,
    A symphony of conformity, where dreams are tucked away.

The weight of generations, a burden on her back,
    A script meticulously penned, a life upon the track.
    Lessons learned in hushed tones, a future etched in stone,
    No room for dissonance, a life forever alone.

The grand piano stands silent, a monument of control,
    Its keys, a battlefield of scales, taking their silent toll.
    Each note a measured whisper, a melody devoid of flight,
    A yearning for improvisation, a symphony bathed in night.

But in the quiet corners, where shadows intertwine,
    A whisper breaks the silence, a spark begins to shine.
    A single, stolen moment, a book with pages turned,
    A world of vibrant colors, where lessons unlearned.

The stories dance and sing of bravery and might,
    Of heroes breaking boundaries, bathed in the morning's light.
    A symphony of rebellion, a yearning to be free,
    A spark ignites within her, a longing to finally see.

The world beyond the castle walls, a canvas painted bright,
    With whispered tales of laughter, and dancing through the
night.
    A world where passion flourishes, and dreams take flight,
    A symphony of possibilities, bathed in the moon's soft light.

The spark within her grows, a ember fanned to flame,
    A secret language blossoms, whispered in her own name.
    She writes in stolen moments, stories yet untold,
    A symphony of defiance, against the world of old.

The rigid lines of expectation, begin to bend and sway,
    As the spark within her grows, a fire that lights the way.
    The practiced smile may linger, a mask she still must wear,
    But the fire in her eyes ignites, a truth beyond compare.

The world may see a phantom, a perfect, polished guise,
    But the spark within her grows, a symphony that will rise.
    One day, she'll break the silence, the cage will crumble down,
    And the spark in the shadows, will light the whole world
around.

For even in the darkness, a flicker can ignite,
A symphony of self-discovery, burning ever bright.
The girl with the hidden fire, will never be subdued,
A spark in the shadows, forever wild and uncdued.

27

The Language of Silence

The world explodes in vibrant hues, a symphony of sound,
　Yet in the heart, a quiet dwells, where emotions unbound.
　No trumpets blare, no drums do beat, a silent, stoic grace,
　A language of unspoken depths, etched on a stoic face.

The weight of years, a heavy cloak, on weary shoulders borne,
　A tapestry of memories, in silence, tightly sworn.
　Joys that bloomed and faded fast, sorrows that linger deep,
　A silent symphony of life, where secrets softly sleep.

The eyes, a well of wisdom vast, reflect a starlit sky,
　Where countless dreams have danced and flown, some soared,
and some did die.
　A flicker of a smile may hint, at battles bravely fought,
　The language of silence speaks, in victories dearly bought.

The gentle touch, a whispered word, a language all its own,
　A warmth that speaks of love untold, a bond that's fully
grown.

No need for grand pronouncements, for empty, fleeting praise,
The language of silence speaks, in the comfort of their gaze.

The furrowed brow, a silent plea, a weight that burdens sore,
A story of unspoken trials, a strength that can't ignore.
The clenched fist, a simmering rage, a fight for what is right,
The language of silence roars, with all its hidden might.

The trembling hand, a silent tear, a grief too deep to share,
A melody of longing lost, a weight beyond compare.
No words can mend the shattered heart, no solace can be found,
The language of silence speaks, in a sorrow most profound.

The world may clamor, shout, and sing, a cacophony of sound,
But in the quiet spaces deep, a truer voice is found.
The language of silence speaks, in every breath, each sigh,
A symphony of hidden depths, where emotions never die.

For silence holds a power vast, a language all its own,
It speaks of love, of loss, of strength, in a language all its own.
So listen to the quiet heart, the whispers in the air,
The language of silence speaks, a truth beyond compare.

28

The Gilded Cage with Silent Bars

Within the gilded cage they built, a symphony goes unheard,
A melody of stifled dreams, a whispered, haunting word.
The polished floors and crystal shine, a facade for all to see,
But the silence screams of battles fought, a prisoner to be.

Her voice, a fragile, trembling thing, long choked by words of scorn,
A constant barrage, sharp and cold, a spirit slowly worn.
With velvet gloves and gentle smiles, the barbs are deftly cast,
Emotional bruises bloom unseen, a torment built to last.

The weight of wealth, a gilded chain, that binds her to this place,
A gilded cage with silent bars, a suffocating space.
Expectations, heavy stones, upon her shoulders rest,
A perfect picture they demand, a life devoid of zest.

The grand piano stands unplayed, its keys a silent choir,
Each practiced note a memory, of passion set afire.
But music's flame, once bright and bold, is dimmed by fear's

cold hand,
   The symphony within her soul, silenced by their command.

In stolen moments, bathed in tears, a melody takes flight,
   A song of anger, hurt, and fear, that bleeds into the night.
   The lyrics whisper of escape, of dreams that yearn to fly,
   A symphony of defiance, a teardrop in her eye.

The opulent decor mocks her, with every gilded frame,
   A constant reminder of the life, they've built to hold her tame.
   The whispered insults, cutting deep, like daggers in the dark,
   Leave scars upon her spirit, a wound that leaves its mark.

But deep within the shattered self, a flicker still remains,
   A spark of fire, a stubborn hope, that whispers through the pains.
   One day, she'll find the strength to rise, above the whispered lies,
   And break the gilded cage apart, with courage in her eyes.

The symphony within her soul, will rise in vibrant sound,
   Shattering the silence, claiming freedom all around.
   No longer will she play their tune, a puppet on a string,
   Her voice will rise, a warrior's cry, a liberated thing.

The world may judge, the world may scoff, at battles fought unseen,
   But the scars she bears, a testament, to the strength that lies within.
   She'll walk away from gilded lies, and build a life anew,
   Where her symphony can finally play, forever bold and true.

For wealth can buy a gilded cage, but it can't hold the soul,
    The human spirit's yearning, to be finally whole.
    And though the path may twist and turn, with trials yet to face,
    She'll find her voice, her melody, and claim her rightful place.

29

The Venomous Symphony

The grand estate, a haunting stage, where shadows twist and turn,
    A gilded cage with velvet bars, where whispers softly burn.
    A symphony of malice plays, a conductor's cruel hand,
    Words like venom, sharp and cold, in a loveless, barren land.

Her voice, a sparrow caught in flight, with wings that clip and fall,
    Each caustic word a searing blow, that tears down every wall.
    "Useless," "failure," "burden," hiss, like serpents in the night,
    Emotional shrapnel pierces deep, extinguishing her light.

The weight of expectations, a crown of twisted thorns,
    A constant reminder of her flaws, a life forever shorn
    Of any love, of any worth, a script she can't fulfill,
    A symphony of degradation, a master's cruel will.

The grand piano stands alone, its keys a mocking choir,
    Each perfect note a distant dream, set coldly on fire.

The music in her heart once soared, a melody so bright,
But drowned by scorn and ridicule, lost in the endless night.

In the dead of night, when shadows creep, a melody takes hold,
A dirge of sorrow, anger deep, a story yet untold.
The lyrics scream of shattered dreams, of a spirit under siege,
A symphony of self-doubt, a prisoner's mournful plea.

The opulent surroundings gleam, a monument to pain,
A constant echo of their power, a relentless, driving rain.
The whispered insults, laced with spite, like acid on her soul,
Leave craters raw and aching, a story left untold.

But buried deep beneath the scars, a flicker yet remains,
A ember of defiance, a fire that burns through chains.
One day, she'll rise above the fray, above the withering word,
Her voice will rise, a storm unleashed, a warrior's battle cry
unheard.

The symphony within her soul, will break its silenced vow,
Shattering the venom's sweet refrain, a truth they can't
disavow.
No longer will she be their muse, to play their twisted score,
Her voice will rise in strength and fury, to rip the silence sore.

The world may turn a deafened ear, to battles fought within,
But the scars she bears, a testament, to the battles she can
win.
She'll walk away from poisoned strings, and build a life anew,
Where her symphony can finally play, forever strong and
true.

For love can mend a wounded heart, where venom sought to slay,
    The human spirit's yearning, for a brighter, better day.
    And though the wounds may ache and sting, with memories that remain,
    She'll find her voice, reclaim her strength, and break the gilded chain.

30

The Atlas Heart

The world unfurls, a vast expanse, a tapestry so grand,
But on her shoulders, burdens rest, a weight of expectations planned.
Not her own dreams, not her desires, a script she doesn't own,
A symphony of other's lives, upon a borrowed throne.

The weight of generations, a crown upon her head,
A legacy to uphold, a path where freedom's fled.
Each whispered word, a binding thread, a future etched in stone,
Leaving the whispers of her heart, forever all alone.

The grand piano stands serene, its keys a silent plea,
Each practiced note a stifled sigh, a yearning to be free.
The scales ascend, a perfect climb, a melody pre-made,
A hollow echo in the room, a soul that's half-decayed.

The lessons learned in judgment's gaze, a constant, watchful

eye,
     Each misstep met with disapproval, a teardrop forced to dry.
     The perfect daughter, friend, and wife, a role she's forced to
play,
     A mask that hides the yearning fire, for a brighter, bolder day.

The weight of expectation, a crushing, heavy cloak,
     Stifles every outburst, every whispered joke.
     A smile plastered, ever bright, a shield against the fray,
     A symphony of hidden truths, with no escape today.

The world demands achievements, a trophy on the shelf,
     A constant need to prove her worth, to please herself and elf.
     But buried deep within her core, a flicker starts to glow,
     A ember of defiance, a seed that wants to grow.

In stolen moments, bathed in dreams, a melody takes flight,
     A symphony of self-discovery, bathed in the pale moonlight.
     The weight she carries, note by note, begins to lose its hold,
     As her own desires take center stage, a story yet untold.

The whispers of her spirit, a chorus starts to rise,
     A battle cry for authenticity, beneath the painted skies.
     No longer will she be confined, by expectations' chains,
     Her voice will rise, a gentle strength, that washes away the
strains.

The world may gasp and question, at the path she chooses now,
     But the symphony within her soul, deserves a brighter vow.
     With every whispered note she plays, a truth begins to shine,
     The weight of expectation, a burden she'll leave behind.

For dreams are meant to be pursued, a fire meant to burn,
  The Atlas heart will find its wings, and lessons it will learn.
  To break the chains of expectation, a symphony to claim,
  And live a life authentically, etched with her own name.

31

The Parchment Heart

The world unfurls in muted tones, a canvas barely touched,
  A symphony of whispered dreams, a story never clutched.
  A life well-lived, a life well-worn, a surface smooth and bright,
  But in the labyrinthine depths, a secret script takes flight.

The parchment heart, a hidden scroll, with ink of deepest blue,
  Holds tales untold, emotions vast, a tapestry brand new.
  Loves unrequited, whispered fears, ambitions set aside,
  A chorus of forgotten songs, the yearnings that confide.

The grand facade, a stoic mask, hides battles fought unseen,
  Victories unsung, and sacrifices, whispered, yet serene.
  Each wrinkle etched, a chapter closed, a triumph or a scar,
  The secret script, a hidden world, beneath a distant star.

The world may see a gentle soul, with eyes that softly gleam,
  But hidden depths hold roaring waves, an ever-shifting
stream.
  A symphony of passions churns, a fire long subdued,

The parchment heart, a silent world, misunderstood.

In stolen moments, bathed in light, the pen begins to trace,
A symphony of hidden truths, on memory's gentle space.
Words flow like tears, a cleansing rain, on pages worn and thin,
The secret script, a whispered song, where life begins to win.

The world may scoff at dreams deferred, at paths they couldn't take,
But in the tapestry of time, a hidden beauty wakes.
For every line etched in the heart, a lesson learned is found,
The secret script, a testament, to wisdom that abounds.

One day, perhaps, the pages turn, the hidden truths unfold,
A symphony of self-discovery, a story yet untold.
The parchment heart, a beacon bright, for those who choose to see,
The hidden depths, the whispered tales, that set the spirit free.

The world may judge a life well-lived, by outward signs alone,
But in the secret script's embrace, a vibrant world is known.
For even lives that seem serene, hold mysteries untold,
A symphony of hidden chapters, waiting to unfold.

So listen to the quiet voice, the whispers on the breeze,
The parchment heart, a hidden world, yearning to appease.
For every life, a story waits, a symphony to write,
A secret script, a world unseen, bathed in eternal light.

32

The Faded Smile and Fractured Glass

In the attic's dusty, shadowed hush, a lonely figure lies,
    A broken doll, with porcelain skin, and faded, vacant eyes.
    Once loved, a cherished childhood friend, a confidante so true,
    Now cast aside, a broken shell, a symbol shattered through.

Her dress, once vibrant, hangs in tatters, a faded, floral gown,
    A crown of tarnished tinsel rests, upon a fractured crown.
    A missing limb, a vacant stare, a testament to time,
    The broken doll, a haunting echo, of a shattered, youthful rhyme.

She held the weight of whispered dreams, and secrets tightly pressed,
    A silent witness to the games, of childhood's joyful test.
    Tea parties shared, and battles fought, with bravery unfurled,
    The broken doll, a loyal friend, within a fragile world.

But time, with unrelenting grasp, has chipped and scraped and

worn,
The once bright colors, dimmed and dull, a faded, sunlit morn.
The laughter's ceased, the games are done, the child has grown and flown,
Leaving the broken doll behind, in solitude to groan.

Yet in her cracks and faded smile, a story can be found,
A symphony of childhood lost, on forgotten, hallowed ground.
The chipped enamel, a silent tear, for dreams that couldn't last,
The broken doll, a monument, to moments fading fast.

Perhaps a child, with curious eyes, will find her in the dust,
And mend her broken limbs and dress, with love and gentle trust.
A thread of hope, a whispered dream, a chance to be reborn,
The broken doll, a symbol still, of lessons love has sworn.

For broken things can hold a grace, a beauty yet unseen,
A testament to memories, of what has always been.
The broken doll, a fragile shell, may hold a heart of gold,
A whisper of a love once strong, a story yet untold.

So let her rest in dusty light, a silent, stoic friend,
The broken doll, a reminder true, that love will never end.
For even in the cracks and breaks, a beauty can reside,
The broken doll, a fragile heart, where love can still confide.

33

The Whispering Blades

The world unfurls in shades of gray, a canvas dull and vast,
 A symphony of muted tones, where vibrant colors cast
 Long shadows in the corners cold, a battle fought within,
 The whispering blades, a constant call, a promise of soft sin.

The polished surface, sleek and sharp, a cruel and tempting glint,
 A promise of release, they sing, a solace in the dint
 Of unseen wounds, of burdens deep, that fester in the night,
 The whispering blades, a siren's song, in the pale and flickering light.

The urge arises, swift and strong, a tremor in the hand,
 To reach and grasp the chilling steel, a desperate, silent command.
 To etch a line across the skin, a crimson, searing mark,
 The whispering blades, a twisted art, leaving their painful dark.

Each mark a story, etched in pain, a language only known
    To the shattered soul that seeks relief, upon a shattered
throne.
    A desperate plea for someone there, to see the hurt within,
    The whispering blades, a silent cry, a symphony of sin.

But in the silence, whispers rise, a chorus soft and low,
    A melody of hope and strength, a seed that starts to grow.
    A voice that speaks of gentler ways, of healing and of light,
    The whispering blades can be defied, and claim a future
bright.

The scars they leave, a constant sting, a reminder of the fight,
    But with each sunrise, comes a choice, to walk into the light.
    To seek the help, the solace true, the strength to overcome,
    The whispering blades can lose their hold, a silent battle won.

The world may seem a canvas bleak, but colors wait to bloom,
    A symphony of self-discovery, dispelling life's dark doom.
    With every tear that gently falls, a promise starts to mend,
    The whispering blades can be replaced, with a love that will
transcend.

There's beauty in the broken things, a strength that can't be
swayed,
    The scars may whisper of the past, but the future can be made.
    Put down the blades, the cutting edge, a path that leads astray,
    Embrace the light, the healing touch, and find a brighter day.

For you are strong, beyond compare, a warrior in disguise,
    The whispering blades can have no hold, with love within

your eyes.
A symphony of hope will rise, a melody so true,
And you will find the strength to heal, and start your life anew.

34

The Canvas of Defiance

The gilded cage, a gilded lie, a canvas preordained,
  With strokes of expectation, where dreams were tightly
chained.
  A symphony of conformity, in muted tones and lines,
  But in the shadows, rebellion stirs, a vibrant spirit shines.

The brushes, cold and rigid tools, hold colors muted, gray,
  A palette of obedience, where passion fades away.
  Scales and portraits, landscapes tame, emotions held at bay,
  A symphony of stifled notes, where melodies decay.

But in the dead of quiet nights, when shadows softly fall,
  A secret brush, a stolen hue, begins to paint the wall.
  A fiery red, a stormy blue, emotions break on through,
  The canvas cracks, the world awakes, beneath a sky of new.

The lines of expectation, once rigid and defined,
  Now twist and turn in joyful dance, a wild and vibrant mind.
  The portraits lose their stoic gaze, their lips begin to smile,

A symphony of hidden truths, defying for a while.

The muted tones, forgotten dreams, reclaim their vibrant spark,
A world explodes in joyous hues, a masterpiece in the dark.
The perfect world, the world of lies, begins to fade and blur,
Replaced by passion, fire, and truth, a world forever pure.

The world may gasp with disapproval, at the colors splashed so bold,
A symphony of dissonance, a story yet untold.
But in the cracks, the beauty lies, in the defiance sung,
A voice that breaks the gilded cage, a spirit forever young.

The artist, once unseen, unheard, now stands with brush held high,
A canvas raised in victory, a truth that can't deny.
This is the world they choose to see, a world where colors reign,
A symphony of rebellion, forever breaking free from chain.

For art can be a weapon strong, a voice that cannot lie,
It breaks the mold, the expectations, and paints a vibrant sky.
The artist's soul, a vibrant flame, that burns with endless might,
A symphony of defiance, a beacon shining bright.

So let the world see their true selves, in every brushstroke bold,
A symphony of rebellion, a story to be told.
For in the heart of every cage, a rebel spirit lies,
And with a brush, a canvas, and a dream, they'll paint their future skies.

35

The Monochrome Mirage

The world unfurls in shades of gray, a vast and endless plane,
A symphony of muted tones, where vibrant colors wane.
The lines are etched in stark relief, a rigid, ordered form,
A stifling monochrome of life, safe from the coming storm.

They walk the path, a marching band, in lockstep, side by side,
Each face a mask, each heart subdued, where individuality
died.
Thoughts echo in the silent halls, a chorus held inside,
A symphony of whispered dreams, where colors long to hide.

The world demands conformity, a tapestry of black and white,
No room for passion's vibrant hues, or individuality's light.
The uniform, a second skin, a symbol of the whole,
Erasing quirks and differences, to reach a single goal.

But in the quiet corners, where shadows softly creep,
A spark ignites, a flicker starts, a promise burning deep.
A single thread, a vibrant hue, a whisper on the breeze,

A symphony of liberation, defying rigid decrees.

The monochrome begins to crack, as doubt begins to bloom,
A yearning for a world in color, dispelling life's dull gloom.
A stolen glance, a whispered word, a secret shared in night,
A symphony of hidden colors, yearning for the light.

A single brushstroke, bold and bright, upon the canvas vast,
A crimson tear, a splash of gold, defying shadows cast.
The monochrome begins to fade, as colors start to fight,
A symphony of liberation, bathed in morning's gentle light.

The world may scoff, the world may stare, at the colors breaking
free,
A symphony of dissonance, a threat to unity.
But in the cracks, the beauty lies, in the defiance won,
A tapestry of vibrant hues, a battle fought and done.

They break the chains of conformity, the mold they once
embraced,
A kaleidoscope of individuality, a future brightly traced.
No longer bound by muted tones, or lines that hold them
down,
A symphony of liberation, where every color's crown.

The world may judge, but they won't turn, from the colors they
create,
A living canvas, ever-changing, defying all of fate.
For in the heart of every soul, a vibrant spirit sleeps,
And with a burst of color, a story boldly leaps.

So let them paint their masterpiece, a world for all to see,
A symphony of liberation, forever wild and free.
For true beauty lies in difference, in every shade untold,
A world of vibrant colors, a story to unfold.

36

The Silenced Choir Awakens

In halls of polished marble, where whispers softly roam,
    A symphony of stifled notes, a melody unknown.
    Each voice, a fragile instrument, with strings that couldn't
sing,
    A chorus trapped in silence, beneath a loveless king.

The weight of expectation, a crown upon their heads,
    A script meticulously penned, a future filled with dreads.
    Lessons learned in hushed tones, a life they couldn't choose,
    A melody of stifled dreams, forever meant to lose.

The grand piano stood alone, its keys a silent choir,
    Each perfect note a whispered plea, a yearning to set fire
    To hearts that slumbered, spirits caged, a symphony unheard,
    A chorus with the power to rise, if only given the word.

But deep within the hidden depths, a flicker came alive,
    A single voice, a trembling note, refusing to connive.
    A melody of self-discovery, a whisper soft and low,

A challenge to the silence, a seed that starts to grow.

In stolen moments, bathed in dreams, the voices start to rise,
    A chorus of forgotten songs, with tears in their eyes.
    The music swells, a tide of truth, that washes over fear,
    A symphony of hidden strength, at last becomes so clear.

The world may judge, the world may scoff, at voices raised in
song,
    But in the cracks of expectation, a new melody is strong.
    The chorus breaks the gilded cage, the silence starts to fray,
    A symphony of individuality, that lights a brighter day.

The music grows, a joyous sound, a testament to fight,
    Of spirits long suppressed, emerging into light.
    Each voice, a unique instrument, a melody untold,
    A symphony of liberation, breaking free and bold.

The world will hear their anthem now, a chorus loud and clear,
    A melody of self-belief, dispelling every fear.
    No longer bound by muted tones, or scripts they didn't write,
    A symphony of true voices, bathed in eternal light.

For in the depths of every soul, a melody resides,
    A song that waits for freedom, where passion gently guides.
    The voices, once unheard, will rise, a chorus strong and true,
    A symphony of self-discovery, forever starting new.

So let them sing their hearts out loud, a melody to share,
    A symphony of possibility, a future bright and fair.
    For in the power of their voices, a truth will come to light,

A world where every melody, takes flight.

37

From Pianos to Stages

In shadows of the dusty room, a grand piano stands,
Its ivory keys, a silent choir, in wait for practiced hands.
A young girl sits, with eyes alight, a melody within,
But fear and doubt, a heavy cloak, that keeps her voice from sin.

The practiced scales, a daily chore, a rigid, structured sound,
No room for passion's vibrant flight, on this forbidden ground.
A tapestry of expectations, hangs heavy in the air,
Dreams of concertos, whispered low, a burden hard to bear.

The world outside, a vibrant stage, with spotlights bright and bold,
Where music takes on form and life, stories powerfully told.
But she's confined to practice rooms, a hidden, secret spark,
A yearning for the open stage, a melody in the dark.

In stolen moments, bathed in moonlight, the fingers softly fly,

Composing whispers of the soul, beneath the watchful sky.
A melody of hidden depths, a symphony untold,
A yearning for a world to hear, a story yet to unfold.

The whispers turn to vibrant chords, a language all their own,
A tapestry of sound and soul, on dreams and passion sown.
The practiced scales, now building blocks, for structures grand and new,
The stage beckons, a distant dream, a shimmering hue.

With trembling hands, she takes a chance, a performance in the hall,
A melody of vulnerability, that conquers them all.
The notes take flight, a soaring song, that breaks the silent hold,
The hidden talent takes its stand, a story bravely told.

The world may gasp, surprised to see, the fire in her eyes,
A symphony that breaks the mold, and shatters all disguise.
The girl who practiced in the dark, now stands beneath the light,
A testament to hidden dreams, that take triumphant flight.

From grand pianos, grander stages, her music fills the air,
A symphony of self-discovery, a journey beyond compare.
The girl who dreamt, the girl who dared, now shares her heart and soul,
An inspiration to all who dream, to reach their destined goal.

For passion thrives in hidden rooms, a melody waiting to bloom,

A yearning for the world to see, a story to consume.
So let the music take its flight, from pianos to the stage,
A symphony of possibilities, etching a new age.

38

The Unveiling

The masquerade, a gilded cage, a mask that hides the core,
A symphony of hidden truths, behind a guarded door.
A performance, practiced well, a role ingrained and worn,
But shadows shift, and secrets stir, a yearning to be born.

The world perceives a stoic form, a portrait cold and clear,
Unruffled by the storms within, devoid of joy or fear.
A tapestry of expectations, a script they hold so tight,
But whispers rise, a hidden fire, that flickers in the night.

The weight of expectations, a burden on the soul,
A constant fight to reconcile, the parts that make them whole.
The yearning for authenticity, a truth that begs to speak,
A melody of self-discovery, a slumbering spirit weak.

In stolen moments, bathed in dreams, the mask begins to crack,
A glimpse of vulnerability, a truth that can't go back.
A brushstroke here, a tear that falls, a layer starts to fade,
The symphony within them stirs, a future yet unplayed.

The heart, a hidden orchestra, with instruments untold,
    Each string a piece of who they are, a story to unfold.
    The courage grows, a tentative step, a whisper soft and low,
    A melody of revelation, begins to gently flow.

The world may stare, confused and shocked, at the one they
thought they knew,
    A symphony of dissonance, a truth that rings so true.
    But in the cracks, the beauty lies, in the vulnerability bare,
    A testament to hidden depths, a spirit taking care.

The mask begins to fall away, revealing all beneath,
    A tapestry of flaws and strengths, a triumph over teeth.
    The world may judge, the world may scoff, at the person
newly seen,
    But in the eyes, a fire burns, a truth that's evergreen.

The symphony within them swells, a chorus bold and bright,
    A melody of self-acceptance, bathed in eternal light.
    No longer bound by borrowed robes, or characters misplaced,
    A symphony of authenticity, forever to embrace.

The world may not understand, the path they choose to tread,
    But in the unveiling's tender light, a spirit finds its stead.
    For who they are, is who they'll be, a truth they hold so dear,
    The symphony of self-discovery, forever ringing clear.

Afterword

This collection of poems is a journey of self-discovery, a melody composed of defiance and dreams. As the author, I'd like to express my deepest gratitude to Steve Johnson from Pexels for the beautiful image used on the cover. The way it captures the essence of rebellion and self-expression perfectly complements the themes explored within these pages.